BMX CHAMP
Acrobats on a Bike

Thomas James

KNOWLEDGE BOOKS

Teacher Notes:

Since its beginnings in California in the 1970s where children started riding their bikes around dirt tracks, the sport of BMX has become hugely popular across the world. It is now an official Olympic sport which involves amazing skills, tricks, and stunts that wow audiences and make kids and adults want to get out there and try it for themselves. Join the author to find out all you need to know to become part of this very popular sport.

Discussion points for consideration:

1. Why has BMX riding and racing become so popular?

2. What are some of your favourite tricks in BMX?

3. Why is it important to be "BMX safe" when riding?

Difficult words to be introduced and practiced before reading this book:

Motocross, motorbikes, balancing, legends, strength, energy, improve, different, explore, muscles, research, safety, important, serious, injuries, reduced, protection, champion, beginner, extras, upgrade, materials, expensive, cylinder, surface.

Contents

1. What is BMX?

BMX means Bike Motocross. Motocross is racing motorbikes on a dirt track. BMX is for racing bikes, not motorbikes.

BMX racing started in California over 50 years ago. The wheel of a normal BMX bike is only 20 inches. It is a smaller bike and suits younger riders.

These days, races take place on a dirt track or in a skate park. The track is made to test your skills. It has hills and turns to push you and your bike to the limit!

BMX riding can be done anywhere. It can be around a small park or yard. The skills of balancing and doing tricks can be practiced over a simple dirt hill.

To start with BMX, buy an old BMX from one of your friends. It is great fun to ride with a friend. You can work on your skills together.

Some friends I know set up a little jump in a garage. It was a very small area. Everyone practiced their jumps and twists.

Do you have a BMX track or skate park close to you? Meet with your friends after school and do some riding. It's so much fun!

You will get to love it and will make lots of friends. You may even see some great legends. You will watch the pros jumping and twisting and think "I will never be that good!" But one day, as long as you keep trying, you will do it!

If you keep trying, you will get better all the time. You may not see yourself getting better, but you are! Your balance, strength, and energy are growing. Practice makes perfect!

The champs that you have seen at the skate park and online have done a lot of work. If you want to improve, think about the move you want to master. Break the move into little steps. If it is not right, think about the steps you need to fix.

2. What Can You Do with a BMX?

There are many different things you can do with a BMX bike. You can go riding with friends and explore along a dirt path. This can be for a whole day or part of a day.

Tell your Mom and Dad what you want to do. They will want to know you are safe and being careful. There are lots of trails for walking and biking in the cities. Stay away from cars and trucks.

When going for a ride with friends, take some food and water. You can carry these in a very light pack on your back. Drink plenty of water as you can sweat a lot.

Biking is tough on the muscles, but you will get very strong. Water and some food will help to keep you feeling good. Be careful if you see walkers. Slow down and be friendly. Give everyone the space they need.

The BMX skate park is a big event. It can even get crowds! This is a great place to go. Go with some friends or meet them at the skate park.

There are plenty of different areas. There are easy areas and pro areas. Start off on the easy areas and keep practicing. Look for a place that looks okay and not too scary.

Now is the time to talk about the moves you will be doing. There are loads of fun tricks that you can research online.

Here are some of the popular tricks:

- The Hop.

- The Drop.

- The Bunny Hop.

- The X-ride.

- The 360 Bar spin.

- The Drop In.

- The 180 Hop.

- The Fakie.

You will learn these tricks if you keep riding and keep practicing!

3. Safety with BMX Riding

The most important thing is to stay off the roads. Cars and trucks move fast and may not see you in time. If you are hit by a car, it will not be a simple fall off the bike. It could also cause a serious injury.

The best idea is not to go on the roads at all. If you ride on the sidewalk or trail, make sure you are not a danger to walkers. Ring your bell when passing.

19

Safety gear is very important to avoid bad injuries. Head injuries can be very serious. They can be reduced by wearing a good helmet.

What is a good helmet? This is a helmet that protects your face, teeth, and jaw, as well as your brain. It may stop serious injuries to your face!

If you fall off the bike at speed, you can hit the ground very hard. Always wear a good helmet! Don't get the cheap ones - your skull is too important!

Besides your helmet, what else do you need? Your knees and elbows will hit the ground when you fall off your bike. If you hit hard, you may even break a bone.

Your hands and knees may scrape along the sidewalk and lose some skin. Skinned knees and elbows are painful! Most injuries are skin rash from the sidewalk or concrete. To reduce skin loss and bruising, wear elbow and knee pads.

23

Do not ride with bare feet. Always put solid shoes on your feet. Tie the shoelaces carefully and very short to stop them getting caught on the bike.

Wear padded gloves to reduce hand injuries. In serious BMX racing, the riders wear racing suits with protection to reduce injuries. The more protection the better!

Being safe is also about how you think. Do not try silly things just to impress your friends!

Always do a slow ride over the track or the skate park first. This will give you an idea of the danger spots or where you may fall off.

Think about the trick you will practice. Then think about how you will escape. This means to work out where you will land if you fall or crash. This escape plan will help to stop you getting hurt. You should always look for an escape plan when you are riding.

4. Buying a BMX Bike

Do you want to buy a BMX? Are you a beginner or a champion? You need to think about these things before buying a BMX.

You can buy a beginner BMX or a champion BMX. There is a big difference in price. Do you need a champion BMX bike when you are a beginner? It would make you look good!

A champion BMX has extras, but these don't matter if you don't have the skills to use these extras. Choose the BMX which helps you to build your skills. You can always upgrade later.

Let's look at the parts of a bike! The first part to look at is the frame. The frame holds the wheels, the seat, the handlebars, brakes, and the person.

The frame is the bones of the bike. If you make the frame out of plastic, would it be able to do Bunny Hops? No, it would break! If you make the frame out of steel, it would be able to do Bunny Hops. Are frames made from any other materials?

A BMX frame made of steel is heavy and strong. BMX frames are also made of aluminum. They are lighter, but also weaker.

Expensive bike frames are made of carbon fiber. Carbon fiber frames are strong and light. A light frame means you can go faster.

Carbon fiber is the strongest and the lightest, but much more expensive. It is made up of coils of carbon fibers mixed with resin. The carbon fiber sheets are stacked together and rolled to form a frame.

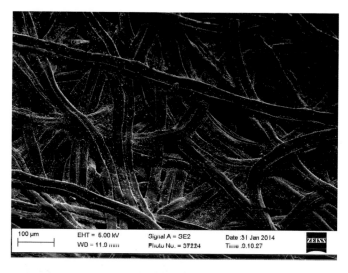

100 μm   EHT = 5.00 kV   Signal A = SE2   Date :31 Jan 2014
          WD = 11.0 mm   Photo No. = 37224 Time :0.10.27   ZEISS

Brakes on a BMX are important for safety. V-Brakes and cylinder brakes allow you to stop very quickly. V-Brakes are great for BMX beginners and less expensive. These work quickly and do not overheat too fast.

The wheels of the bike are made up of spokes and tires. Tires on a bike need to be able to hold on to the surface. Smooth tires will cause your bike to slip and fall over.

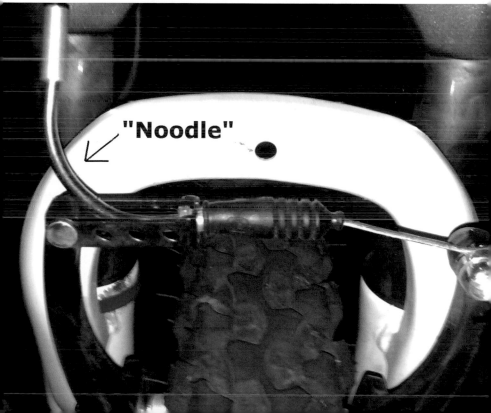

"Noodle"

5. Looking After Your BMX

A good bike will last a long time if it is looked after. How do I look after my BMX?

Keep your BMX in a dry place. Do not let water drip on to the bike. Water will cause the BMX to rust. If you store it in a dry place, it will not rust.

Clean all the mud and dust off your bike. If you wash your BMX with soap and water, you will also remove the oil.

Oil is used to help the moving parts turn easily. It also stops the metal parts from heating up too much.

Spray oil onto all the moving parts of your bike. This includes the chain, the gears, and the moving parts of the wheel. Wipe off the excess oil from these parts. Do not let oil drip on the frame or the tires of your BMX.

The chain of your BMX must be kept clean and firm and oiled. If the chain becomes loose, it will fall off or break. Always check the chain before riding and keep it free of dirt and dust.

The chain on a BMX will loosen with all the heavy use caused by doing tricks. You need to undo the bolts on the frame and tighten the chain. The chain will last a long time if you check it and keep it firm, clean, and oiled.

Tires on a BMX are mostly very wide. These tires help in doing tricks like hops and jumps. The tires grip on to the surface very quickly. Their wide size gives them a bigger grip.

When you are starting with a BMX, it is best to get a tire that will help you to ride easily and not slip. The tire should have a good tread to grip the surface. It is now time to get out and have some fun on your BMX!

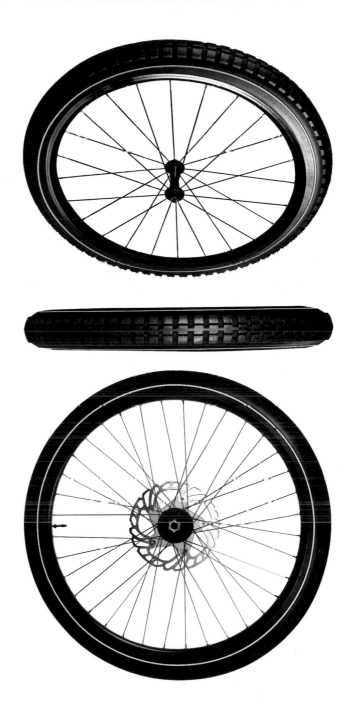

Word Bank

Motocross

motorbikes

balancing

legends

strength

energy

improve

different

explore

muscles

research

safety

important

serious

injuries

reduced

protection

champion

beginner

extras

upgrade

materials

aluminum

expensive

cylinder

surface